Original title:
Ripples of the Blue

Copyright © 2025 Creative Arts Management OÜ
All rights reserved.

Author: Henry Beaumont
ISBN HARDBACK: 978-1-80587-358-7
ISBN PAPERBACK: 978-1-80587-828-5

Lullabies from the Deep Blue

In the ocean's embrace, fish laugh and play,
Tickling the waves in a silly ballet.
Jellyfish jiggle, doing the twist,
While crabs hold a dance-off, none can resist.

Starfish lounging on rocks like a king,
Sing tunes of the sea, oh what a thing!
Seashells echo their giggles and glee,
Under the moon, it's a grand jubilee.

Horizons Weaving Through Water

Mermaids gossip, with fins in a swirl,
Sharing the latest on seaweed and pearls.
Crab in the corner, he's quite the clown,
Telling tall tales of waves breaking down.

Octopus twirls in a jolly parade,
With eight arms waving, he's not being played.
Fish wear top hats, quite dressed for the show,
In this watery carnival, laughter will flow.

Touching the Dusk of the Oceans

Dolphins decide to start a new trend,
Twirling their tails as they dive and bend.
Whales throw parties with bubbles galore,
While sea turtles glide in and out of the door.

The sea anemones bounce to the beat,
With a bounce that's fun, oh what a feat!
Jellyfish serve snacks, what a sight to behold,
Swaying with laughter, their jiggly mold.

The Azure Realm Beneath the Waves

Clams share secrets in their shells so tight,
While lobsters pinch jokes that are quite a delight.
Schools of fish swim in comical loops,
Bumping and giggling, joining the groups.

Coral reefs sparkle, a colorful view,
With sponges that giggle, and laughter arrayed too.
In this underwater party, joy is the key,
Where the nonsense and fun flow so free!

Tides of Celestial Azure

The ocean danced in joyous play,
A fish wore sunglasses, what a display!
Seagulls sang with a comical flair,
While crabs strutted like they had no care.

A dolphin twirled, doing a jig,
While turtles laughed, a hilarious gig.
The seaweed swayed, like it had a tune,
Under the bright and cheeky moon.

The Sapphire Serenade

In a pool of laughter, the splashes soared,
A mermaid sneezed, and everyone roared!
With buckets of giggles, in colorful hues,
The starfish wore hats, it's quite the ruse.

Octopuses danced in a conga line,
While squids played tag, oh how divine!
With bubbles popping like a playful show,
The sapphire waves felt the laughter flow.

Waves of Tranquil Turquoise

The turquoise water held a raucous scene,
A crab sent selfies, looking quite keen!
With turtles on surfboards, they took the plunge,
As gulls yelled "Catch me!" in a fun-loving lunge.

The fish tried yoga, a pose called the twist,
But most just flopped, oh the humor missed!
As hermit crabs raced in their tiny shells,
They cheered for each other, with laughter that swells.

Submerged in Cobalt Dreams

In cobalt waters where the silliness reigned,
A whale told jokes, while the others just strained.
The coral sat gossiping, adding some flair,
While clam shells chuckled, all snuggled in there.

With octopus juggling and fish doing pranks,
The sea was a circus, filled with hoots and shanks!
As the waves splashed secrets, they flickered with glee,
Beneath the cobalt dome, was pure jubilee!

Flow of the Aquatic Serenade

In the pond, the frogs croak tunes,
Dancing fish in flashy costumes.
Turtles sunbathe, strike a pose,
While ducks don hats, as laughter grows.

Koi fish dress in scales of gold,
Jokes fly by, they never grow old.
A catfish tells a knock-knock joke,
While bubbles rise, like giggles woke.

A snail moves slow, yet steals the show,
With a shell so bright, watch it glow.
The water's lively, full of cheer,
No room for gloom, just fun down here.

Bubbles giggle, splashes chime,
In this world, we dance through time.
So join the fun, don't miss the beat,
The pond's a stage, it's quite a treat!

Secrets Beneath the Turquoise Veil

Underneath the waves, there's chatter,
A clam's retort, "Hey, what's the matter?"
Octopus plays cards, with tricks to spare,
While seaweed wiggles, what a flair!

Crabs gossip quick, with sideways moves,
A dolphin shows off, it grooves and grooves.
Starfish whisper gossip in the sand,
They giggle so hard, they can't quite stand.

A turtle wears shades, thinking it's cool,
While jellyfish start their own school.
The seashells snicker, as tides go by,
In the aquatic realm, no reason to sigh.

A seal rolls over, jokes on repeat,
With fins in the air, this life is sweet.
So dive on in, don't fear the spin,
Underneath the waves, let the laughter begin!

Lullaby of the Mystic Marsh

In the marsh, the crickets sing,
Frogs add to it, what a thing!
The fireflies blink in disco light,
While owls hoot their jokes at night.

Mudskippers hop, a comical sight,
With wings of jest, they take to flight.
A heron stands tall, trying to pose,
But trips on a stick, and down it goes!

The reeds whisper secrets, soft and sly,
As dragonflies buzz by, oh my!
Tadpoles giggle, blowing tiny bubbles,
In this marshy realm, it's all just fun and chuckles.

So come dance with the shadows, join the tune,
Laughter echoes beneath the moon.
In the marsh, where joy is saved,
Every moment's a giggle, forever engraved!

Currents of the Azure Whisper

In the gentle flow, fish spin around,
Splashing water, what a sound!
A shrimp's in a tutu, doing the dance,
While a pufferfish tries its luck at romance.

The anemone giggles, no denying,
As clownfish jest, all the while flying.
Crabs build castles, enjoy their reign,
Yet sneaky seagulls swoop in for the gain.

The corals gossip about a fish's new hue,
And even the rocks laugh, their sides turning blue.
A whale makes a blunder, singing off key,
While dolphins unite, laughing with glee.

With every wave, the humor flows,
In this aquatic land, where laughter grows.
So take a dive, or simply sway,
In the currents of fun, come out and play!

Either Side of the Deep Aqua

In a pool made of jelly, not quite real,
Swimmers slip and slide with vibrant zeal.
Rubber ducks can quack but can't take flight,
While we splash about till the end of the night.

Fish wear sunglasses, they swim with style,
Bubbles can giggle and dance for a while.
Laughter echoes where silly seas meet,
While we try to juggle our drinks and our feet.

Interludes in the Water's Dance

A dolphin spins in a watery-spin,
Grinning like it knows where we've been.
Mermaids giggle with a playful tease,
Offering snickers with a splash of breeze.

Dive down deep where the seaweed sways,
Octopuses play games that last for days.
With tickles and wiggles, they start a show,
In masks made of shells, we cheer and glow.

Discovering Depths of Serenity

Beneath a calm sea, a crab tells a joke,
Waves roll in laughter, it almost chokes.
Turtles bob gently, not in a race,
While starfish sit grinning, they're really quite ace.

Blowfish puff up at the fun-filled sight,
Making us giggle with all of their might.
The ocean's a party where everyone's sly,
As we swim through chuckles that ripple and fly.

Traces of Turquoise Memories

We found a treasure in sandcastles tall,
Built from the laughter that came with a call.
Seashells whispered secrets of days gone by,
While seagulls squawked jokes and flew in the sky.

Each wave brought tidbits of humor and grace,
Floating on rafts, we all found our place.
With lemonade laughter and cupcakes on deck,
Salty breezes carried our joy on the speck.

Reflections of the Wandering Wave

A fish in a bowler hat,
Swims by with a rolling chat.
"Is that a wave in your pocket?"
"No, just my lunch and a locket!"

The seagulls wear shades of flair,
They squawk while combing their hair.
"Got any fries?" one suddenly squeaks,
"Only the ones that taste like leaks!"

A crab tries to dance in a line,
To music played from the brine.
He slips, he trips, oh what a scene,
Now he's grumpy and covered in green!

Underwater a clam tells a tale,
Of how he got caught in a gale.
"I opened my shell wide one fine day,
For a pearl party gone quite astray!"

Choreography of the Cobalt Tide

A dolphin with moves like a pro,
Shows off a backflip and a throw.
"Who needs a pool when you've got style?"
"Just watch out! Here comes a wild tile!"

The octopus leads the parade,
With arms in a synchronized cascade.
"Don't get algae stuck in your toes!"
"At least give a wink to the rose!"

Bubble parties are quite a sight,
Balloons float up, oh what a flight!
With laughter that tickles the sea,
Even the seaweed joins the spree!

A walrus slides into the mix,
With clumsiness and silly tricks.
"Join me in this frolic and dance!"
"Just watch your step, there's no second chance!"

Harmonies of the Glistening Tide

A sea star sings with pure delight,
Under the moon's silvery light.
"Do you know any sea shanties true?"
"Only about fish that can't chew!"

The jellyfish floats like a song,
With tendrils that dance all day long.
"Is this a party or a float?"
"Just don't get caught in my coat!"

A turtle with shades on his face,
Takes his time in a lazy race.
"Fastest swimmer? Oh what a joke!"
"I'll win with style, you little bloke!"

And dolphins in a conga line,
They wiggle and laugh, feeling fine.
"Who needs trouble when we just groove?"
"Let's start a wave, let's make a move!"

Veils of the Wandering Waters

A mermaid lost her favorite veil,
Said it sailed away with the gale.
"Who knew tides could be so bold?"
"Perhaps it danced with the gold!"

Fish in tuxedos parade around,
Hosting a ball without a sound.
"Will you dance?" one fish does tease,
"Only if you wash your fins, please!"

The sea sponge joins with a slow spin,
Propelled by a giggle under skin.
"Is this a dance or a bubble bath?"
"It's both! So join my batty path!"

A whale brings the beats with a thrum,
All the sea life starts to hum.
"We're the best hosts, can't you see?"
"Just don't compare us to land debris!"

Underneath the Twilight Current

Fishes wear sunglasses, so cool,
Dancing in circles, breaking the rule.
Seahorses gossip like old chums,
Chasing the bubbles, here come the drums.

Crabs do the cha-cha on sandy floors,
While dolphins giggle, opening doors.
With shells as hats and laughs in the air,
The ocean's a party, without a care.

Oracles of the Endless Horizon

Octopus psychic predicts a splash,
A jellyfish giggles, it's quite the bash.
Starfish concoct a plan so sly,
To jump in the air and wave goodbye.

The gulls are making bets on the side,
Who'll land the best, it's quite a ride.
With seaweed cape, it looks so funny,
The fishes plot, and oh, it's sunny!

The Rhythm of the Aquatic Soul

Every wave sings a silly tune,
The turtles groove to a funky moon.
Eels twist and turn in a comical style,
Making the sea chuckle, oh what a while!

Clams throw a party, pearls in a pile,
Zebras and seahorses dance for a while.
With krill as confetti, laughter erupts,
In this aquatic scene, mischief corrupts!

Shadows Danced on Gentle Waves

The shadows sway like a shifty prank,
As fishy shadows play in a plank.
Mermaids giggle with hair full of sea,
Throwing a conch shell, calling with glee.

A narwhal's trumpet sends ripples of joy,
While grinning dolphins dance without coy.
With a splash and a swish, all creatures unite,
In the dance of the waves, a hilarious sight!

Enchantment From the Water's Edge

A sprightly frog took a leap,
Hopping high, making fish weep.
With a laugh and a splat,
He swam off with a hat.

The turtles danced, oh what a sight,
With silly moves, they brought delight.
A dolphin joined in with flair,
And spun 'round like it just didn't care.

The seagulls cawed, feeling bold,
As they told tales of treasures untold.
"They found a shoe and a tin can lid,
And oh, that frog, he really just hid!"

Bubbles burst, and laughter rang,
While the waves played a silly tang.
The water's edge was pure bliss,
As creatures shared a jovial kiss.

A Symphony of Deep Teal

Underwater, the fish hold a show,
Clowning around, putting on a glow.
A goldfish plays a shiny flute,
While starfish dance in warm pursuit.

Seaweed sways to the funny tunes,
As octopuses ride their brooms.
Crabs clicking claws in time with glee,
"More fun than napping under a sea!"

A lobster's wiggles bring forth a cheer,
He slipped on a shell, landed near.
"I promise I'm a dancer, not a fool,
Just try not to slip in this salty pool!"

Jellyfish glow, illuminating the night,
Making shadows that twist and take flight.
In this symphony, joy reigns supreme,
Giving laughter the loudest esteem.

Beneath the Veil of Indigo

A wise old squid wore a grand cape,
Telling jokes while he shaped a grape.
"Why did the fish go on a diet?"
"Because it found scales too tight!"

In the indigo depths, where light plays,
Bubbles rise, in whimsical displays.
Seahorses tumble, doing ballet,
"A pirouette is easy when you sway!"

Anemones giggle, swaying no less,
Tickled by visitors in their address.
"Come join our dance, oh what a thrill,
Just watch your step or you'll trip on a bill!"

The ocean chuckled, both far and wide,
As creatures shared humor, side by side.
In every nook, laughter cascades,
Unraveling fun that never fades.

Echoing Through the Water's Heart

A dolphin whistled a tune so sweet,
Chasing bubbles like a running feat.
Dancing through currents, oh what a scene,
With splashes and laughs, he was quite the dream.

A pufferfish puffed up with pride,
Worrying fish who tried to hide.
"Look at me, I'm a balloon!
But don't let the catfish see too soon!"

Giggling clownfish painted in stripes,
Played hide and seek in their funny types.
With each turn, they squeaked joyfully,
Painting the waters, oh how they'd agree!

Through murky depths and sunlit shine,
The heart of the sea was feeling divine.
In these echoes of laughter's embrace,
Every creature found its unique place.

Chasing the Turquoise Shadows

In a pool of playful tides,
Fishes wear their goofy grins,
A crab in shades bumps his ride,
While seaweed sways and spins.

Gulls dive down with silly flair,
Splashing storms of feathery cheer,
The ocean's laugh fills the air,
As shells giggle, 'We're all here!'

A turtle sneezes, makes a wave,
The bubbles pop—they dance with glee,
And every wave, so bold and brave,
Turns serious thoughts to a spree.

With sea stars wearing tiny hats,
And dolphins chasing sea kite strings,
The turquoise shadows hold their chats,
As laughter floats on finned-up wings.

Twilight Hues in the Deep

A sunset blinks with colors bright,
As octopus plays peek-a-boo,
The seabed sparkles, a silly sight,
With jellyfish in costumes too.

A clam sings out with a silly twang,
While starfish clap their arms in cheer,
The comical dance of fins that fang,
In twilight's hues, they have no fear.

With mermaids brushing on their scales,
And dolphins playing with the moon,
All sea creatures swap silly tales,
While crabs go dancing to a tune.

Even the darkness has a joke,
As laughter bubbles from below,
In the deep where shadows cloak,
Twilight's hues make spirits glow.

The Dance of Marine Whisper

With a swish and a splash, the sea breaks out,
Fish don their slippers, oh what a sight!
Glimmering whispers that giggle about,
As conch shells echo jokes late at night.

A flounder flops, trying to glide,
While sea cucumbers try to slide,
Waves of laughter float on the tide,
Marine ballet, a goofy ride!

Turtles in tandem with laughter abound,
Synchronized to the ocean's beat,
They do a slow dance that spins round and round,
With seahorses bouncing on soft, sandy feet.

The floor of the sea, a theater grand,
Fish in tuxedos, they take their chance,
Crashing to the shoreline, they form a band,
With giggles and grins, they all dance!

Horizon's Whispering Surface

On the edge where the sea meets the sky,
Splashing water tickles sandy toes,
Seagulls gossip as they glide high,
While sunsets dress in rosy clothes.

Waves toss sprightly, clapping their hands,
As beach balls bounce in a carefree spree,
Crabs in a conga, they dance on the sands,
The horizon hums a silly decree.

A lighthouse beams, wearing a grin,
With lanterns flickering tales of cheer,
As the tides weave stories of chaos and kin,
While driftwood drummers make all revere.

Under twilight's embrace, fish play a game,
Seeking the spotlight, creating dispute,
In whispers of mirth, their laughter aflame,
With each wave's rise, the giggles shoot.

Embraced by the Sky's Reflection

The fish wear tiny hats this day,
Dancing in circles, making quite the play.
A frog in a tux hits the dance floor,
While ducks quack tunes, asking for more.

The clouds giggle, shaping silly sights,
As crickets chirp under moonlit lights.
The breeze joins in, swirling around,
Tickling the trees, making them sound.

Lakes of Luminous Light

In a lake where the glowworms compete,
A turtle does yoga, isn't that neat?
The lilies wear hats, bellflowers sing,
While dragonflies flaunt their colorful wing.

A fish tells a joke, the crowd all guffaws,
While frogs sip tea, applauding with paws.
The sun winks down, throwing sparkles in,
As laughter erupts; oh, what a din!

Beneath the Twilight Turquoise

The otters are sliding on slippery slides,
A seagull's still learning, it flaps and glides.
Stars join the fun, twinkling in delight,
As crabs put on shows, under the starlight.

The ripples are laughing, making a ruckus,
A clam throws a party, and who can resist?
With fish playing tag and the moon on display,
Who knew such silliness lived by the bay?

Chasing Echoes on Liquid Canvas

A painter of bubbles splashes with glee,
Making portraits of frogs, oh such artistry!
The wind carries laughter, a symphony bright,
As shadows paint stories in the fading light.

A crab conducts music, waving a claw,
While minnows swim past with a fabulous awe.
The water shimmers like a critter's mirth,
Cheering the funnest show on this earth!

Reflections on Aquamarine Waters

A fish with a hat swims by,
Winks at me with a fishy sigh.
I drop my snack, it's pure delight,
He grabs my chips, what a fishy fight!

Seaweed dances, waving 'hello',
A crab takes a selfie, puts on a show.
Oh, sandy toes and squawking gulls,
Join the fun where the water pulls!

The turtles gossip in bubble chat,
While dolphins dance with a playful splat.
A jellyfish floats with a jiggly grin,
Be careful, don't poke! He might just sting!

The splash of a wave, a humorous drench,
Turns me around in a playful wrench.
But laughter echoes up to the sun,
In waters that sparkle, the joy is spun!

Shimmering in the Ocean's Embrace

A seal in sunglasses, oh what a sight,
Sipping his drink, feeling just right.
He raises a paw, invites a toast,
To all the sailors, he loves the most!

Bright crabs march with a sassy strut,
While seagulls flirt, it's quite the glut.
An octopus joins, wearing a bow tie,
Making everyone laugh, oh my, oh my!

The tide brings in giggles from afar,
As waves crash in like a bizarre bazaar.
A fish parade with glittery scales,
Happily dancing with the wind in their tails.

With every splash, a burst of cheer,
The ocean laughs, it's crystal clear.
In this shimmering world, let's play and sing,
Under the sun, life's a funny fling!

Serene Azure Reflections

Breezes whisper, the surf does chat,
A seagull giggles while wearing a hat.
Underwater, a clam cracks a joke,
Everyone's laughing, letting joy soak!

Fish in tuxedos spin round and round,
While starfish cheer from the sandy ground.
A splash of fun, what a quirky sight,
In this azure world, where day meets night.

The shrimp host a party, colorful and bright,
With conch shells singing, everything's right.
Toot your own horn, come twirl on the wave,
Where each bubble's a giggle, and joy is the rave!

With crabs on the dance floor, boogying free,
And mermaids chuckling in harmony.
Here in this realm of splashy delight,
The sea is a stage, life's a joke outright!

Cascading in Celestial Waters

In a pool of giggles, the fish take a dive,
A whale tells a tale that's sure to revive.
The sea stars applaud with glowy delight,
As barnacles grin, this feels just right!

With bubbles that pop like a crisp party cheer,
The ocean's a stage for laughter so clear.
A dolphin spins tales, with antics galore,
As crabs crack up on the golden shore.

Each wave carries whispers of funny tales,
Of squids in top hats and fish dressed as snails.
The chorus of seagulls strikes a fun note,
As jellyfish twirl, like a party afloat!

Gleeful giggles reflect in the tide,
In this watery world, we sparkly glide.
With every splash and every swirl,
Life is a riot in this ocean girl!

Dreaming in Seafoam Dreams

In the splash of a wave, a sea creature grins,
With bubbles of laughter, where the fun begins.
A starfish in shades, doing the cha-cha,
While octopus plays tunes on a seaweed guitar.

The crabs hold a race, oh what a sight,
With shells like lightning, in the sparkling light.
They dance with the jellyfish, bouncing around,
In a waltz on the sand, without making a sound.

Ocean's Embrace at Dusk

Seagulls are gossiping, what a delight,
While whales tell tall tales under the night.
A dolphin flips high, then lands with a splash,
And fish form a conga, oh how they dash!

The lazy old turtle, with a wink and a grin,
Says life's like a party, just let the fun begin.
As the stars twinkle down in gentle parade,
Under this sky, no one's ever afraid.

Translucent Moments in the Tides

A crab with a hat, how quirky and small,
His friends in the tide pool are having a ball.
A shrimp pulls a prank, with a splash of surprise,
As the seashells just roll their beady old eyes.

Bubbles keep popping, like laughter afloat,
With sea urchin jokes that tickle the boat.
The sun's golden rays turn the water to gold,
Where fishes sing ballads, both funny and bold.

The Veil of Pristine Waters

In waters so clear, where the mermaids do play,
With laughter that echoes through night and by day.
A crab in a bowtie, he gives quite a show,
While the sea cucumbers steal snacks from below.

Pearls giggle together, they're a cheeky bunch,
While a whale brews coffee for all at lunch.
The currents they twirl, like dancers so free,
Sending giggles and grins from the depths of the sea.

Where Dreams Dip Below

In a world where fish wear hats,
And swim in line for scatty chats.
They gossip 'bout the lure that glows,
And how they danced on squishy toes.

A crab who thinks he's quite the star,
Recites his lines from near and far.
With claws like jazz hands, full of flair,
He moonwalks past the jelly glare.

There's a turtle with a funky tie,
Sipping seaweed tea as time floats by.
He speaks of tides and wild sea spins,
Laughing 'bout the chaos that begins.

So when you dive, don't just take a look,
You might meet a fish that really cooks.
Their underwater jokes, so slick and bright,
Will spin your worries out of sight.

Through the Lens of Aquatic Dreams

Through goggles thick, I see the dance,
A whale doing the hula, what a chance!
With bubbles popping, laughter spills,
The ocean's comedy, full of thrills.

A dolphin flips in perfect glee,
Wearing sunglasses, oh so carefree.
As sea cucumbers tell dad jokes,
The clownfish chuckle, raising strokes.

Fins are twirling in glittering sights,
As sardines perform their acrobatic flights.
They whirl and swirl, a slippery crew,
Singing in harmony, a watery hue.

So dive deep, bring your funkiest hat,
Join the aquatic laugh fest, imagine that!
With a splash and a giggle, we'll float away,
As the ocean's jesters brighten the day.

The Secret Life of Liquid Hues

Beneath the waves where secrets lie,
Colorful fish wear ties and sigh.
The seahorses play cards with flair,
While octopuses braid their hair.

Anemones squeal as they sway,
Dreaming of the beach on a sunny day.
A starfish lays and takes a nap,
Counting jellyfish, what a trap!

Clownfish paint their faces bright,
Before they dive into the night.
They throw a rave beneath the foam,
Where every fish can find a home.

So peek below, don't just float,
Join the fun, grab a fishy coat.
Together we'll dance in a swirl of hues,
Laughing with fish in joyful views.

Mystic Melodies Beneath the Surface

With a splash, the bass start to sing,
While sea turtles do their wing-a-ding.
The underwater band plays a tune,
As they dance 'neath the silly moon.

A shrimp on drums keeps the beat,
While a flounder shuffles on its feet.
Mermaids cheer in flowing gowns,
While waves giggle in playful downs.

The seaweed sways like a magic wand,
A rhythm found in the ocean's grand.
Even the clams join in the fun,
Chanting choruses just for one.

So come along, let's make a splash,
In this aquatic world, we'll surely dash.
With laughter ringing through the deep,
In mystic melodies, we'll always leap.

Lattice of Liquid Light

In the pond, frogs leap and croak,
Belly flops make the lilies choke.
Fish exchange their witty grins,
While ducks plot splashy little sins.

Sunbeams dance on water's sheen,
Jellyfish jelly-laugh, so keen.
The otters slide, then go 'whee!'
Pretend to surf, they're so carefree!

Giggling waves, a playful fight,
The turtles race with all their might.
Silly splash and silly sound,
Nature's laughter all around.

Dances in the Indigo Current

Mermaids twirl in seaweed veils,
While seahorses tell tall tales.
A dolphin drags a beach ball through,
Cracking jokes that might be true.

Octopuses juggle, what a sight!
With eight arms, they're quite the fright.
Clams hide pearls with giddy glee,
Taking bets on who will flee.

Waves break with laughter loud and bright,
The ocean's party feels so right.
Starfish pop with laughter, too,
Spilling secrets of the blue.

Breath of the Serene Surface

On still lakes, ducks don't even pout,
They're too busy swimming about.
Tourists spill chips, quite a mess,
While pigeons make their bold excess.

Tiny boats bob like little bugs,
Giving cozy nudges and hugs.
The geese play charades on the shore,
Flapping wings for a little more.

The water's calm, but funny flies,
Make silly shapes that mesmerize.
A frog in shades, a king so grand,
Rules his pond with a wave of his hand.

Canvas of Celestial Reflections

Stars twinkle down on waves that shimmer,
While fish put on their nightly glimmer.
A catfish croons a catchy tune,
While crickets chirp to the glowing moon.

Clouds drift in with a fluffy cheer,
Playing peek-a-boo for all to hear.
Bubbles float like little dreams,
Bursting giggles in sparkling streams.

The night is bright with laughter's spark,
Fireflies twirl, a glowing arc.
In this liquid canvas, hearts ignite,
As nature dances in sheer delight.

Hues of the Hidden Abyss

In the depths where creatures play,
A fish with shades of pink and gray.
He winks and does a little twirl,
While dancing with a dizzying whirl.

A clam wears pearls like a phony crown,
Claiming he's the brightest in the town.
But watch out for the lobster's laugh,
He'll pinch your ego in a photograph!

When seaweed tickles just right,
The jellyfish joins in for a fright.
They boogie down with a jig and a sway,
Turning the tide into a cabaret!

An octopus taking the lead,
With eight left feet, oh what a breed!
Each step is a slip, a slide, a plop,
He's the star of this aqua flop!

Sway of the Sapphire Sea

The waves giggle as they crash,
Bubbles popping in a splash.
A dolphin plays a game of tag,
With a turtle, who goes, "Frog!" and drags.

Seagulls squawking, trying to sing,
They can't hold a note, what a thing!
While crabs compete for the best dance,
Shaking their claws in a prance.

The sun's high, casting silly shadows,
On starfish in sun hats, looking like fellows.
They try to surf on jelly bean waves,
But end up tangled like colorful braves!

Fish gossip in bubbles of glee,
Sharing secrets, oh, did you see?
The sea cucumber, dressed to impress,
Looks more like a mess than an address!

Murmurs from the Ocean's Heart

The tide whispers tales of the day,
Where sea monsters wish they could play.
A mermaid with hair made of kelp,
Sings songs that make fish yelp!

A crab with a monocle takes a seat,
Sipping seaweed tea, a rare treat.
He chuckles at fish in a make-believe race,
While sea urchins giggle at every disgrace.

Coral reefs hold a dance of their own,
With tiny shrimp throwing a groovy bone.
They twist and twirl, and loopy they go,
As anemones sway to the show!

Shimmers in the Crystal Depths

Glimmers sparkle like a hundred jokes,
Where sea creatures tease with their pokes.
A whale shares puns that echo far,
While changing his shirt to a rainbow star!

The sea cucumbers chuckle in line,
While chowing down on some old brine.
They toast to the waves and their silly ways,
Wishing for laughter to fill all their days.

Seahorses gossip about tides and moon,
As silly dolphins sing lullabies in tune.
Each splash they make creates a swirl,
In a dance party beneath the pearl!

Beneath the Canvas of Waves

In the ocean's grand show, we wade,
Where jellyfish do a wobbly parade.
A crab in a tux, what a sight to see,
Looks like he's heading to tea, with glee.

Fish gather 'round for the grand buffet,
With seaweed pasta, oh what a way!
Octopuses dancing, moving so slick,
Yet still, they trip on a floating old stick.

The sea turtle struts, thinking he's cool,
While seagulls squawk like they're still in school.
Bubbles rise up, looking quite cheeky,
And the dolphins laugh, oh how they're sneaky!

So here we shall dive, what a vibrant scene,
With spectacles daily, both silly and keen.
Under the waves where the fun won't stop,
Beneath the waves, we all do flip-flop!

When Cobalt Winds Whisper

When breezes chuckle and seashells laugh,
A dolphin dons shades, what a funny half!
Seagulls gossip about fishy affairs,
While crabs share secrets, with none who cares.

Waves tell jokes that only they know,
Telling tales of mermaids in flamboyant flow.
The turquoise tide rolls in, bringing surprise,
With a fish on a skateboard, reaching for the skies!

The stars cheer on as they shine and twinkle,
Each splash of humor makes our hearts crinkle.
Sandcastles tumble from laughter so bright,
As we giggle along with the moon's gentle light.

In this cobalt world, every joke's a delight,
With waves full of laughter, oh what a sight!
So let's ride the surf on this funny spree,
Where the sea and the sky join in jubilee!

Illuminated by the Sea's Gift

In twilight hours, the fish wear their best,
In glittering scales, they dance, never rest.
With a starfish DJ, spinning the tunes,
And a clam that sings, oh how it croons!

Squid paint the waters with colors so bold,
While waving to turtles, both young and old.
Shy little shrimp throw a shrimp cocktail bash,
Inviting all sea life for a splashy splash!

Jellyballs jiggle, with laughter they bounce,
As barnacles chuckle, doing their pounce.
The seaweed grooves, swaying left and right,
Under the moon's glow, it's a sight so bright.

So let's toast with conch shells to this quirky glee,
For in the ocean's arms, we all feel free.
With humor aglow, like lanterns afloat,
In the sea's treasure chest, expect joy to gloat!

The Final Tides of Day

As the curtain falls on the ocean's ballet,
The fish take their bows in a shimmering spray.
With a clam in a hat, and a crab with a cane,
They strut on the sand, like it's all just a game.

Waves start to giggle, as the sun dips low,
With tales of the day, they happily flow.
Sea turtles munch popcorn, and watch the bright show,
While dolphins do flips, in the last warm glow.

The moon winks softly, casting silver beams,
Painting the sea with whimsical dreams.
A starfish belly dances, what a fine way,
To wrap up the laughs of this splashing day.

So as the tides whisper their goodbyes and cheer,
Let's treasure these moments, with laughter so near.
For every tide that comes, with its playful display,
Leaves us with chuckles, as we drift away.

Whispers Across the Water

A fish wore a hat, oh what a sight,
I laughed so hard, it took flight.
Splashing around, the frogs tried to sing,
But all that I heard was a rubber band fling.

The ducks quacked jokes, how silly they were,
One tried stand-up, but he lost his spur.
Water lilies giggled, petals all bright,
In this splashy comedy, what pure delight!

A turtle went surfing—what a bold quest,
With a shell that glistened, he thought he was best.
The waves gave a chuckle, with salty cheer,
As he paddled along, forgetting his fear.

Oh, the pond was alive with the silliest crew,
In a world full of giggles, it's hard to be blue.
With every soft ripple, a chuckle did swell,
In this watery circus, I bid you farewell!

Echoes of the Deep

The octopus danced in his funky attire,
His moves were so quirky, you'd think he'd retire.
With eight wiggly arms, he wobbled with style,
Making all the fish smile, just for a while.

A clam tried to sing with a voice like a bell,
But it sounded like someone who tripped in a well.
The seaweed all swayed, keeping perfect time,
To the underwater boogie, a bubbly rhyme.

The starfish chimed in, with a joke so absurd,
"Why don't sea monsters ever say a word?"
"Because they're all shy, and they hide under rocks,
When the waves start to dance and they hear the tick tocks!"

Echoing laughter spread far and wide,
In the depths of the ocean, where giggles abide.
Creatures of whimsy, all swirling around,
In the ebb and the flow, happiness found!

Serenade of the Silver Waves

The seagulls composed an outrageous song,
While barnacles bobbed, tagging along.
Each note had a splash, each chorus a cheer,
Even the crabs clacked, can you hear?

A dolphin sprang up with a graceful twist,
"Jump in the fun, you surely can't miss!"
With bubbles in tow, and a wink of the eye,
He led all the sea life in a sprightly fly-by.

Anemones giggled, lost in the flow,
As jellyfish glimmered, stealing the show.
They bounced to the rhythm, all floaty and free,
In the shimmering concert, come join the spree!

The currents all danced, in a sea full of glee,
With laughter and music, there's joy for the sea.
So let's twirl and swirl, don't leave me alone,
In this aquatic gala, let's all find our home!

Tides of Tranquil Dreams

The whale had a dream of flying so high,
But his wings made of bubbles just floated on by.
With every big splash, he giggled and sank,
In the warm ocean blue, what a laugh-filled prank!

A crab in a bow tie was making a toast,
To all of his friends, he liked them the most.
"Let's eat some seaweed, it's the finest cuisine,
With a sprinkle of salt, it's a culinary scene!"

The sunfish rolled over, eyes all aglow,
"Who needs a beach when you've got a show?"
With reflections of wonder, the sea sparkled bright,
In the tranquil tides, it felt just right.

So dance with the bubbles, and sway with the tide,
Let laughter surround, let your joy be your guide.
In the ocean's embrace, may your worries all cease,
In these whimsical waters, find laughter and peace!

Emotions in a Sea of Blue

Waves dance with laughter, oh what a sight,
Fish wear bow ties, creating delight.
Seagulls juggling chips under the sun,
Even the crabs join in on the fun.

Sandcastles boasting, "Look at my height!"
Seashells tell tales of a party last night.
Starfish play piano on their sandy stage,
While dolphins dance, free from any cage.

The tide pulls a prank, splashing the shore,
A walrus in shades makes the beach roar.
Everyone giggles at the ocean's great tease,
As jellyfish wear hats with flamboyant ease.

Beneath Stormy Currents

Clouds roll in, but don't start to fret,
Octopuses knitting, you won't forget.
Whales hosting karaoke, a true sensation,
Singing 'Under the Sea' with grand ovation.

Umbrellas flip, like fish in a race,
Turtles in flip-flops just keep up the pace.
A thunderous roar turns to giggles galore,
With a storm of jellybeans washed up on the shore.

Lightning flashes, but it's just for the show,
Sardines applying for a talent flow.
A disco floor opens with bubbles and cheer,
As the ocean sparkles, it's party time here!

Murmuring Shadows of the Tide

In the depths where the seaweed sways cheerfully,
Mermaids flip coins, wishing for glee.
Crabs tell knock-knock jokes to sea urchins near,
All of them giggling, sipping on beer.

Silhouettes dance while the night softly hums,
Ghostly fish wearing their fanciest sums.
Under the surface, the laughter's like wine,
Each bubble a giggle, sparkling divine.

Shadows of sharks play a game of charades,
With the most epic antics of oceanic spades.
Sardines dress up, pretending to be,
A little rock band with a guitar of sea.

Navigating the Ocean's Heart

Sailing along the whimsical stream,
Fish with binoculars plotting a dream.
A seagull as captain, with a glitzy hat,
Directing the crew, even a fat cat!

Mermaids at the helm, flipping their tails,
While jellyfish wave in their colorful sails.
Every wave whispers secrets of cheer,
As laughter erupts from the ocean's great ear.

Surfboards giggle, joined in the race,
Chasing the sun with a splash of grace.
In the currents, the fun never departs,
Navigating joy with the ocean's warm heart.

Horizon's Elegy in Blue

A fish swam by with a quirky grin,
It swirled and twirled without a spin.
The seagulls laughed at its silly show,
While the sun shone bright, putting on a glow.

The waves rolled in like a silly dance,
They splashed around in a frothy prance.
A crab in a tux made its formal way,
Said, "Excuse me folks, it's my ball today!"

A dolphin popped up with a flip so grand,
Said, "Catch me if you can! Come grab my hand!"
But slippery luck had him dart away,
Now he's pondering mooching a beach cabaret.

The horizon chuckled, with clouds as a hat,
Waves bowed low like a comical spat.
Life's a grand sketch in shades of delight,
At sunset, even fishes will dance through the night.

Awakening the Cerulean Soul

The ocean yawned, stretched its arms so wide,
It tickled the toes of a starfish inside.
With laughter like bubbles, the sand made a joke,
"Why do we sunbathe? Because we love the yolk!"

A jellyfish floated with a flair so bright,
Claiming each wave as its dance floor tonight.
A turtle, confused, stuck its head in the sand,
Wondering where all the party bands planned.

Seashells conspired, each with a tale,
Of ships that went missing, with no chance to bail.
They giggled and gossiped till dusk turned to dawn,
As seaweed chimed in, in a jazzy yawn.

Then seagulls swooped in, with snacks from the sky,
"Bargain lunch ahead! Let your troubles fly!"
And so the sea's mirth echoed far and near,
In a world where humor would always steer.

When the Waters Came Alive

On a sunny day when the tide rolled in,
A dolphin yelled, "Hey, let's have some gin!"
The ocean replied, with a splash and a glee,
"Sure thing, my friend, but not too much sea!"

Crabs donned glasses as they sipped from seashells,
While fish joined in singing aquatic carousels.
A clam brought the beat, with a thump and a clap,
As they served up cocktails in a bubbly whirlpool lap.

The starfish found rhythm, tapping its feet,
While a whale played a song that was funky and sweet.
Octopuses twirled, lost in the groove,
Dancing wild like no one had anything to prove.

The surf called for water, "Wave up a cheer!"
As they boogied and wiggled without any fear.
And so the waters laughed in their joyous revel,
In a tidal parade, bright fun on the level.

Dancing Light on the Surface

A flick of the fin, and the sunlight gleamed,
While plankton twinkled as though they dreamed.
Little fish joked, playing tag with the rays,
"Catch me if you can, in this playful maze!"

The water sparkled, alive with delight,
A shark passed by, with a grin so bright.
"I'm not scary, just seeking some fun,
Join me for a swim under the sun!"

A school of fish flitted, a colorful show,
Their brilliant scales made the current glow.
"We're the shimmering stars of the ocean's floors,
Underneath the waves, we open all doors!"

And as day turned to night, the moon took its place,
Casting silver beams on fish in a race.
With laughter and joy, in the ocean's embrace,
Time dripped like honey in this whimsical space.

Essence of the Ocean's Palette

The waves are dancing with glee,
A fish just sneezed, oh, can't you see?
An octopus wearing a tiny hat,
Crab's playing cards with a friendly rat.

Seagulls singing in off-key notes,
Jellyfish wearing bright pink coats.
Turtles glide in a silly race,
The sea is a canvas, a funny place.

Flight over Sapphire Waves

Up in the air, a seagull pranks,
Dropping snacks into the fish tanks.
A dolphin leaps, strikes a pose,
While the starfish plays the piano with toes.

On a surfboard, a seal tries to spin,
End up crashing; oh, where's the win?
The waves are chuckling all around,
As laughter echoes, joy is found.

Journey Through Azure Vortex

In a whirlpool of giggles and fun,
A clam's new dance has just begun.
Worm deciding to crawl or to hop,
A merry-go-round that never will stop.

With each turn, the colors collide,
As fish tell jokes on the joyous ride.
It's a sea circus, wild and bright,
Where every splash brings pure delight.

Beneath the Shimmering Surface

Bubbles rise like whispers of cheer,
A crab in a tutu starts to appear.
The coral's laughing, it's quite a show,
As clowns dive deep for the pearl below.

A sea cucumber flexing with pride,
Cheering on minnows in a funny slide.
A treasure chest opens—what's the surprise?
Just another fish with big, googly eyes!

The Allure of the Ocean's Caress

A jellyfish wobbles, oh what a sight,
Floating like it's in a dance, quite light.
Seagulls squawk gossip about the tide,
While crabs decide who's got the best stride.

With beach balls bouncing and sand in toes,
A child draws a castle, but off it goes.
The waves crash in, it's a game of tags,
As sunscreen slips—oh, the friendship brags!

Beach umbrellas flit, like fish in a net,
Sandy snacks turned to grainy regret.
Flip-flops are lost, they float out to sea,
Chasing them down? Now that's just sheer glee!

Sunburns and laughter, a recipe bright,
Ocean mischief from morning to night.
Each splash and giggle writes stories anew,
In this salty mess, we find joy so true.

Pulses of the Celestial Flow

Stars in the sky are just fish on a hook,
Casting wishes, come take a good look!
The moon grins wide, with his silver spoon,
Stirring tides and giggles, all night till noon.

Turtles play tag with the drifting light,
While dolphins do flips, oh what a delight!
The cosmos chuckles, a celestial show,
As comets zoom past, in a humorous flow.

A jellyfish wiggles, it tickles the sea,
Bubbles rise up, it's a fizzy spree.
Celestial light bounces off fishy scales,
Making each wave tell whimsical tales.

The waves don their hats, a fine seaside wear,
Wobbling and bobbling, they dance everywhere.
Under this blanket of sparkly glow,
The universe laughs, as below they flow.

Whispers of the Azure Dawn

Morning beams peek through the sleepy waves,
Seashells are gossiping, oh, how it braves!
The crabs exchange jokes about the tide,
While fish in their schools do a synchronized glide.

A pelican's dive—what a clumsy show,
Plunging for breakfast but comes up with… whoa!
The tidepool's full of stories to tell,
With sea urchins laughing, they cast their spell.

Seagulls squawk loudly, a raucous affair,
Combing the beach like they own the fair.
The laughter spreads wide as the beachcombers scurry,
For treasures unearthing brings wild, funny flurry.

Sunshine breaks out, crabs wave goodbye,
As sea cucumbers do a slow, silly sigh.
The day's just begun, oh the fun that it brings,
In this humorous dance, let joy take to wings!

Echoes in the Indigo Depths

Indigo waters hum a playful tune,
Where mermaids giggle beneath the bright moon.
Octopuses juggle, a fantastic act,
And sea horses prance in their colorful pact.

Pirates on surfboards are searching for gold,
But all they find are tales to be told.
The seaweed sways, a dancer at night,
While starfish argue on the best way to bite.

The whales burst forth in a symphonic cheer,
Singing the sea's songs that only we hear.
Clownfish in coral throw a wild bash,
Bubbles and laughter, oh, what a clash!

At last, we dive in for a splashy time,
In these depths of humor, it all feels sublime.
Each wave tells a joke, each splash shares a grin,
Echoing laughter, let the fun begin!

The Calm Before the Cerulean Storm

In the ocean's silent hum,
Jellyfish dance, a whimsical drum.
Gulls snicker overhead, quite sly,
As waves plot mischief, oh my my!

Bubbles burst with giggles, you see,
A sand crab juggling, oh so free.
Fish wearing hats swim past with glee,
Some even twirl in a bizarre spree!

A dolphin slips on seaweed tight,
A seal gives a wink, oh what a sight.
Winds share secrets, a playful tune,
All is well on this sunny afternoon!

Dreamscapes in Marine Blues

Mermaids sip tea from clam-shell cups,
While starfish giggle, doing jump-ups.
The sea turtles race on a whim,
And octopuses play hide and swim.

Crabs hold disco parties at dusk,
With conch shells blasting, it's quite a fuss.
They tango on reefs, full of zest,
While sea cucumbers take a rest.

Coral gossip spreads wide and fast,
'Have you seen the blubbering whale, so vast?'
Waves chuckle at all this hubbub,
Life's a laugh beneath the sea rub!

The Aquatic Rhapsody

A fish with a bow tie swims with flair,
While sea horses gossip without a care.
The dolphins serenade the squirrely rocks,
With laughter echoing through the flocks.

Clams wear pearls like a crown so bright,
Playing dress-up in the dappled light.
Turtles reading books with shells adorned,
In a world where silliness is never scorned!

Bubbles laughing, they tickle the fins,
As sea otters play games, oh what wins!
Underwater laughter, a joyous sound,
In a realm where silliness knows no bound!

Shadows of the Deep Sea

Down in the depths, shadows twist and jig,
A pufferfish pouts, 'I'm not a bigwig!'
Anglerfish grins with a lightbulb glow,
Sardines squabble in a choreographed show.

Ghost crabs moonwalk on silvery sands,
While jellyfish glide on their translucent hands.
Anemones laugh, tickling fish galore,
In their underwater carnival, never a bore!

The squid throws ink like it's confetti,
Scaring the blues while keeping it petty.
With a splash and a giggle, the ocean weeps,
For it's never too serious in the deep's funny keeps!

Serendipity in Ocean's Breath

A fish wearing glasses swam by a feather,
He quipped about jelly, 'Let's see if it's better!'
Turtles danced funny, quite bold and quite brazen,
While seahorses giggled, the ocean was blazin'.

A crab told a clam, 'Your shell is so nice!'
The clam just turned pink, and said, 'What's the price?'
A dolphin jumped high, with a splash and a spin,
Said, 'I'll take my coffee with salt and a grin!'

Starfish played poker on sun-kissed rocks,
While octopuses laughed, playing tricks with their socks.
The tide brought in humor, with waves full of cheer,
In this wacky blue habitat, all were sincere.

So let's raise a toast to the life on the shore,
Where laughter is plenty and good times galore.
With each wave that rolls, let the fun multiply,
In the ocean's own breath, where the silly fish fly.

Beneath the Veiled Waves

In shadows of seaweed, the sea cucumbers sleep,
They dream of adventures in waters so deep.
A clam whispered softly, 'Did you hear that great joke?'
'It's about a great whale who thought he was smoke!'

An eel with a wink danced through the kelp,
Said, 'Life is electric, come join, give a yelp!'
The fish in their colors sparkled quite bright,
As they shared all their secrets, with sheer delight.

Anemones floated, all dressed up in style,
They swayed to the rhythm, in a glorious file.
A dolphin proposed, 'Let's play hide and seek!'
But the turtles just chuckled, 'You know we're not sleek!'

In the dance of the tides, joy bubbled and burst,
With laughter around, it was truly well-versed.
Underneath the salty skies, mischief takes flight,
Where friends of the ocean find humor in light.

The Touch of Turquoise Light

A starfish with style wore shades, quite supreme,
Declaring, 'I'm famous; I'm living the dream!'
A flounder swam by, held his breath just in case,
He slipped on a sea mat, and fell with great grace.

The sea turtles chuckled, 'Oh, dear, what a sight!'
While crabs did a cha-cha, oh, what pure delight!
Bubbles burst laughing, like secrets we share,
As sea urchins rolled past, with spines in the air.

A dolphin popped up, shouting, 'Have you seen my new hat?'
A pelican replied, 'Let me guess, it's a flat!'
The coral all giggled, with colors so bright,
In the glow of the turquoise, the laughter took flight.

So dance with the waves, let your silly heart glow,
In this fun underwater, just let yourself flow.
With laughter like bubbles, let merriment bloom,
In the depths of the ocean, joy chases the gloom!

Shaping the Symphony of Blue

From the depths of the ocean, a tune softly played,
A whale with a banjo serenaded the shade.
Shrimps joined the chorus, tap dancing with glee,
While sea frogs croaked bass notes, quite brilliantly.

The sea urchin grinned, with his spikes all aglow,
He tapped on a conch, keeping time in the flow.
A starry-eyed fish spun in circles with flair,
While crabs clapped their claws, filling up the cool air.

The tides kept a rhythm, waves slapping the sand,
Echoing laughter, making moments so grand.
A playful young dolphin flipped high in the air,
Yelled, 'Catch me if you can, if you dare, if you dare!'

In the symphony's heart, all creatures unite,
With giggles and splashes, oh what a delight!
So join in the dance, let the music imbue,
In this whimsical ode of the shimmer and blue!

www.ingramcontent.com/pod-product-compliance
Lightning Source LLC
Chambersburg PA
CBHW051735290426
43661CB00123B/453